£ 5.95

Legal Weapon II

by Mark Wheeller

dbda

Legal Weapon II
by Mark Wheeller

"Legal Weapon" was commissioned by:
Bedfordshire, Berkshire, Buckinghamshire, Cambridge, East Sussex, Essex, Hertfordshire, Isle of Wight, Kent, Oxfordshire, Surrey, Suffolk and West Sussex County Council Road Safety Departments.

Author's acknowledgments:

Ian Harris, Principal Road Safety Officer, Oxfordshire County Council Road Safety Group; Mandy Rigault, Senior Road Safety Officer, Oxfordshire County Council Road Safety Group; Mike Pill, Area Commander, Oxfordshire Ambulance Service, NHS Trust; Meg Davis and Sophie Gorell Barnes of MBA Literary Agents for their continued interest in my work; Tony Audenshaw and Matt Kane of Ape Theatre Company for their imaginative ideas to improve on my original script.

All the characters in this play are fictional although accounts of Road Traffic Accidents/ Offences are devised from those with first hand experience of Road Traffic Accidents.

Published as Legal Weapon by *dbda* in 1999
This updated and revided edition, published by *dbda* in 2005

ISBN 1 902843 01 0

BRITISH LIBRARY CATALOGUING IN PUBLICATION DATA
A catalogue record for this book is available from the British Library.

All enquiries regarding all rights associated with this play, including performing rights, should be addressed to:
Sophie Gorell Barnes, MBA Literary Agents Limited, 62 Grafton Way, London W1P 5LD.
Tel: 020 7387 2076   Fax: 020 7387 2042   E-mail: sophie@mbalit.co.uk

Further copies of this publication can be purchased from:
dbda, Pin Point, 1-2 Rosslyn Crescent, Harrow HA1 2SB.
Tel: 0870 333 7771   Fax: 0870 333 7772   E-mail: info@dbda.co.uk

If I am asked to write a Road Safety play, I always jump at the chance. There is lots of scope for dramatic moments, fast action and opportunities to utilise a variety of dramatic conventions and presentation techniques. By their very nature, they require an imaginative response to write and stage the climatic accident scenes. Beyond that there is a great sense of satisfaction and fulfilment in knowing that in addition to them being "exciting theatre" they do help to reduce accidents and save lives.

Legal Weapon arose out of a request from Mandy Rigault and Ian Harris from Oxfordshire County Council Road Safety Department to write a play about the dangers of speed. Their phone call came to me out of the blue and was the first time I'd been "commissioned" to write a play... to be performed primarily by school or Youth Theatre Groups. A number of other counties subsequently chose to become involved in the commission. I was over the moon!

The main rule I have applied to writing my Road Safety plays is that they should be good stories, and open to imaginative presentation. They should be plays that I, as a Drama teacher, would want my GCSE groups to benefit from seeing. The (crucially important) Road Safety element should add to an already interesting story and set of character relationships.

Mandy Rigault organised some interviews with people who had been convicted of serious road traffic accidents where speed was a contributory factor. The interviews were planned to happen on one day. By lunch time I was feeling a bit down... each of the three people who had come forward to talk to me stressed that their main charge had been drink/driving. The ideas were therefore covering the same ground as those explored in *Too Much Punch For Judy.* After lunch, a very confident and charming young man walked into my interview room keen to tell his story. He applied the most unexpected argument to the circumstances of his accident. Although he openly admitted he was speeding (70 miles an hour in a 40 zone), he claimed that he did not **cause** the accident which led to the death of a motorcyclist. In his view the motorcyclist was responsible for her own death because she pulled out of a junction... without looking. He was very eloquent in his justification and was able to gloss over the fact that, according to the

Introduction

investigation, it was unlikely that she would have been able to see him when she looked in his direction before pulling out. His speed was such that he would not have been visible over the brow of a hill. Although upset by the death, he was more upset about being in prison. It was the experience of prison that would stop him from ever speeding again.

This unexpected perspective provided me with the main body of the story. I sat at my word processor and invented a love triangle story (which I had never done before and wanted to try) assimilating road safety messages into that structure. I also had another objective; to create a scene which could be used by GCSE drama students to present in their final performance exam. Section 4 of the play attempts to fulfil this. The final conflict between Andy, Jazz and Matt was written with the GCSE requirements in mind: five minutes per performer, with a cast of more than two. That part of the play is 15 minutes long approximately, and has good roles for one female and two male actors.

The play was due to be premiered by a number of schools from the commissioning Counties on the same day. One of the schools (my old school St. John's, in Epping, Essex) somehow got permission to do a private performance the week before the official premiere, so that by a strange quirk of circumstances I saw that version first. I was invited to watch it in the same Drama studio as **Too Much Punch For Judy** had first been performed under my direction nearly ten years previously.

This performance was excellent. There are many bits that I had forgotten about and so, at times, I was pleasantly suprised by the script as well as the little touches that had made sections "come alive". My main reaction was: "Wow! That's a relief! It does hang together... it does work!".

The following year my own Youth Theatre membership requested to do the play. My relationship with the play became much closer during our rehearsal period and I made a number of changes.

One major challenge is staging a car accident with limited resources. I remember that I had brought eggs and melons to the rehearsal with the vague notion that battering them with a piece of metal would somehow represent the idea of metal hitting flesh. Try as we might... none of these ideas worked out! Suddenly we hit upon the idea of Andy actually beating

Kelly (the motorcyclist) up... on and on... mercilessly... relentlessly... in the same way that a car will continue on its path no matter what is in its way. Andy was in control of the car, so in essence it was he who was driving this metal at Kelly. We found a way of staging the initial impact and then followed it up with a merciless slow motion one-on-one beating. The idea worked brilliantly and I can remember going home very excited about it.

When a week later I went to see the *Ape Theatre Company's* professional premiere, I discovered they had used a similar way of conveying the violence of the accident. How both groups came up with such a "new" idea, working in two different parts of the country... I shall never know!

Ape Theatre Company (who continue to tour **Too Much Punch For Judy** so successfully after ten years) took on the professionally touring rights to this play throughout England. Tony Audenshaw and Matt Kane, the directors of *Ape* proposed a change which I couldn't imagine working. It has since become one of my favourite aspects of the play. Their idea was to open the play with a seemingly irrelevant snippet of conversation, taken from the middle of the script. I could not see any way to make this work until I saw the *Ape* performance. The idea was excellent and I immediately adopted it and drafted it into the script.

The *Ape* production was way beyond my expectations. What I really liked about it was how much they'd added to the script without actually changing the words. This is best exemplified by their use of vocal sound effects made throughout the play to create various atmospheres and moods. There are so many other examples I could give. I was absolutely gob smacked! If you have seen their touring production you will know exactly what I mean. I consider myself to be very fortunate indeed to have had the opportunity to see my work enhanced by top professionals... and this version of the script benefits enormously from their input.

Coming back to the play three years after its conception to prepare for its publication has been a joy. Elements of the play pleasantly surprised me... and some of it even made me laugh. I've made a few more alterations for this, the published version of the play. I hope it finds its way into lots of School/College Drama departments and onto lots of school stages.

Good luck with any work you choose to do with it.

Introduction

April 2005

To date **Legal Weapon** has been performed 1897 times. There's an old phrase "if it ain't broke... don't fix it." I have never felt that it was "broke(n)", but when faced with the temptation of giving it an overhaul I couldn't resist! This arose because dbda had unearthed some research findings suggesting that young people respond more positively to Road Safety messages when the offender knows the victim. In **Legal Weapon** (I) Andy does not know his victim. I seized on this opportunity to both re-draft the play (there are MANY changes in this new version... many "upgrades") and incorporate the idea of Andy knowing Kelly. This factor adds considerable "drama" to the climatic Section 4 and I'm pleased with the result and look forward to seeing it on stage. (If you do present the play... let me know... if at all possible I will try to come and see it!

Working on this play after so many years away form it has been intriguing. There were times when I thought... "that was clever!" as I read it. There were equally times where I thought... "how on earth did that get into the original published script?" This serves to re-enforce what I always say to my own GCSE groups... a play is never finished, it is always ongoing. So, here is the current version of Legal Weapon, retitled **Legal Weapon II**. It really is a different and "much improved" play.

Mark Wheeller

6

Cast List

When performed by a cast of four, it can be done in the following manner:

Female 1:	Cath MacFarlane; Jazz Mainah; "A"; Clowns/Masks; Neighbour 1; B-D; Paramedic 2 & 3; Witness.
Female 2:	Kelly MacFarlane; "A"; Clowns/Masks; Police 2; Prisoner 2.
Male 1:	Andy Bowen; "A"; Clowns/Masks.
Male 2:	Matt Irvine; "A"; Clowns/Masks; Police 1; Car Salesperson; Neighbour 2; Paramedic 1; B-D; DI Morris; Prisoner 1.

This play should be performed with minimum props
and maximum imagination!

The professional premier of Legal Weapon was
by Epping based Ape Theatre Company
in January 1996.

The cast was as follows:

Andy: Shaun Dooley
Jazz: Julie Nicholson
Matt: Kyle Harris
Cath: Susan Mitchell

Directors:

Mat Kane & Antony Audenshaw

Section 1: Love's Young Dream

(A slide, or a banner, at the back of the stage reads:
"Human blood is heavy; the man that has shed it can not run away." *African proverb.*
This should be in view as the audience walk in to the auditorium. It can remain in view throughout the whole play but should be lit throughout the whole of Section 4 and as the audience leave.
Very loud music plays. Cathy, Kelly's Mum, is offstage. Kelly puts on her coat, shoes and rucksack ready to go out.)

Kelly: Mum!

Cathy: *(Off)* What?

Kelly: Can you lend me a fiver… petrol for moped. Interview at the supermarket. Remember?

Cathy: Forgot... sorry.

Kelly: Pay you back when I get the job!

Cathy: *(Entering, and getting the money from her wallet.)* What if you don't?

Kelly: He already said he liked the look of me!

Cathy: You watch him. *(She gives Kelly the money.)*

Kelly: Thanks Mum. *(Kisses her. Picks up [from A] a cheap and much used motorcycle helmet.)* I'll be back as soon as I can... just after five I guess. *(Kelly freezes.)*

Cathy: *(Momentary pause.)* Good luck Kelly. *(Freeze)[1] (Silence)*

A: *(Enters, looking at, or touching Kelly.)* Disposing of someone by crashing into them is easy, although there are other ways of committing murder:

Clowns/Masks enter accompanied by appropriate pre-recorded or live music, vocal sound effects and/or gobbledygook speech. Feel free to

---

[1] *Thanks to Ape Theatre Company who'd suggested this should be at the start of the play. I remember saying… "It'll never work!"*

Section 1

develop this opening idea. Start off with a bang! In the Ape Theatre Company production, amplified vocal sound effects were used throughout the whole production to great (comic and dramatic) effect.

Two Clowns/Masks come forward. One has a large inflatable club. The other is unarmed. UNARMED walks around nonchalantly. CLUBBER, tiptoeing behind him/her clubs UNARMED who falls to the ground. CLUBBER continues to club UNARMED mercilessly – a premonition of the car crash in Section 3(?). Meanwhile GUNMAN – dressed in Western gear, with appropriate music in background – creeps up behind CLUBBER. CLUBBER finishes clubbing, checks UNARMED is dead. Puts his/her club down, brushes hands together, turns and is shot by GUNMAN with a very loud shotgun.)

This, of course, is only pretend.
(The Clowns/Masks come back to life.)
In real life it is advisable not to kill people.
If you do...
(One Clown/Mask strangles another)
... expect to be outcast by Society...
(Mime showing how – the other clowns outcast STRANGLER.)
No, it's much more fun to... *(Pre-recorded orchestral music floats in and the Clowns/Masks change their mood)*... fall in love...
(mime: Clowns/Masks falling in love)
This happens to our protagonist... Andy...
(Enters, as the Clowns/Masks exit.)
... and the current object of his desire... Jazz.
(Jazz enters.)
Whenever they see each other, their pupils dilate *(Mime)* and strange feelings pass through the whole... yes the whole of their body. *(Mime!)*
Finally, they pluck up the courage to ask each other out. *(Simultaneously both take a breath to ask the other out.)*

Both: I... *(They stop. Embarrassed silence.)*

Jazz: Yeh?

Andy:	I... erm... I don't really know why I'm here.
Jazz:	What?
Andy:	Aren't you gonna ask me?
Jazz:	What?
Andy:	Why I'm here!
Jazz:	Tell me!
Andy:	'Cos I was beamed up.
Jazz:	Beamed up?
Andy:	One minute I'm eating my lunch... the next "Pow!" I'm here! Weird eh?
Jazz:	Very weird!
Andy:	Never happened before... just "Pow!"
Jazz:	"Pow?"
Andy:	Actually Jazz, I walked here. *(Indicating legs)* On these... both of them... like this. *(Demonstrates a "walk".)* Piece of piss really!
Jazz:	And?
Andy:	I came to ask you... *(Clearing his throat, preparing for asking her out)* How... *(finally chickens out)*... Aaaargh!
A:	Asking someone out is not much more fun than being killed! *(Another murder in the background?)*
Jazz:	Do what?
A:	Come on. Big deep breath and...
Andy:	Jazz... *(Suddenly becoming very melodramatic)* There's something I need to say to you.
Jazz:	Are you trying to ask me out?

Section 1

Andy:	I've been waiting for the right… *(Suddenly double taking on Jazz's previous line)* What did you say?
Jazz:	If you are, the answer's yes!
Andy:	Cool!
Jazz:	Where shall we go?
Andy:	*(Andy fumbles, stutters, stammers for a long time before saying quite decidedly!)* You choose.
Jazz:	Clubbing?
Andy:	My dancing's embarrassing; I look like a Fimble[2] on acid. *(Appropriate over the top mime!)* How about Bunjee jumping?
Jazz:	*(Laughing)* I can't even do long jump!
Andy:	A meal… you're not on a diet are you… not that you need to be… I mean…
A:	What will they do?
Both:	*(Very loudly)* Aaaaargh!
A:	Idea! *(Tongue in cheek)* Ping!
Both:	*(To each other)* How about the Cinema?
Andy:	*Fatty Fearful II* is on!
Jazz:	Sounds good.
Andy:	Or *Romantic Movie III*?
Jazz:	*Fatty Fearful II* eh?
Andy:	I'll pick you up…
Jazz:	Seven o' clock.
Both:	Date! *(Jazz exits.)*

---

[2] *Or other topical cultural reference.*

Andy:	*(Fx. Atmospheric sound. Andy speaks as though entranced. His delivery becomes deliberate.)* A motorbike is a very macho thing. Throttle up and you're away. The brute power all there and you're in control of it. It's taming that power I like. The feeling you're on the edge of control.
Jazz:	Kell! You'll never guess what?
Kelly:	Andy Bowen finally asked you out?
Jazz:	How do you know?
Kelly:	He asked me first.
Jazz:	What?
Kelly:	*(Laughing)* No… what I thought you'd say…
Jazz:	And?
Kelly:	I said you were gagging for it!
Jazz:	I am!
Kelly:	So's he. He's like a little boy. Well nervous! Where're you going?
Jazz:	Cinema.
Kelly:	On his bike?
Jazz:	Yeh.
Kelly:	You seen it?
Jazz:	Not the new one.
Kelly:	Cool or what? Which film?
Jazz:	*Fatty Fearful II*
Kelly:	Rubbish!
Jazz:	Who cares! *(Both laugh as they exit.)*

Section 1

A: Seven fourteen that evening… Andy arrives, the neighbours' curtains twitching, *(Faces appear from different points/levels from behind curtains/screens all over the stage area.)* as his monstrous machine throbs outside Jazz's home.

Jazz: My dad's having a fit!

Andy: You weren't expecting a "ride" on something as big as this then?

Jazz: *(Laughing)* Size isn't everything!
                  How does it handle?

Andy: I can coax it in the most slippery of conditions!

Jazz: *(Tapping watch)* Shame it couldn't get you here on time!

Andy: I was round Grandad's.
                  (Passing motorbike helmet to Jazz.)

Jazz: *(Jazz puts on her motorcycle helmet)*
                  That's really sweet.

Andy: Nan died, about a month ago.

Jazz: He's on his own then?

Andy: Yeh, he's like a dad to me. I help him do up cars… have done since I was a twinkle in my dad's pants.

Jazz: Andy!

Andy: *(They both laugh.)* Come on…

Jazz: What time does the film start? Quarter to?

Andy: Half-past.

Jazz: *(Looking at watch in horror.)* Will we make it?

Andy: No problem!
                  (They get on the bike. Fx. ignition.)

Both:	Throttle. *(Engine roars.)* Go!!! *(Possible use of pre-recorded music, as they speed off on the bike.)*
Jazz:	*(Sudden transition.)* Whoo! What a ride!
Andy:	What a film!
Jazz:	What an evening!
Both:	What a start to our relationship!
Jazz:	*(With horror)* What a journey home!
Andy:	*(Looking at watch, musing.)* Ten minutes to get here... home in eight and a half eh? Piece of piss!
Jazz:	What?
Andy:	Just a game... *(Subtle use of atmospheric fx. To be said with significance. Turning to audience in slow motion.)* ...adds interest to the journey.
Jazz:	Game?
Andy:	*(To audience with significance.)* A battle, between the bike, the road and me. The race instinct. It's not unusual. *(Fx. off.)*
Police:	Nee nah! Nee nah! Nee nah! Nee nah!
Andy:	Oh no!
Police 1& 2:	'Ello 'ello 'ello 'ello! What's going on here then?
Andy:	*(Taking off helmet. Jazz leaves hers on.)* Just driving home after an evening out Officer.
Police 1:	Not been drinking I hope.
Andy:	No Officer. I don't do that.
Andy & Jazz:	*(To audience)* It's dangerous!
Police 2:	In a hurry?
Police 1:	What speed were you doing?

Section 1

Andy:	Normal for this road, Officer. Built up area. Thirty?
Police 1 & 2:	Professional are you?
Andy:	What?
Police1 & 2:	Comedian! *(They laugh then turn on Andy becoming more menacing.)* This says you were doing fifty.
Andy:	*(In a very high pitched voice.)* Fifty? Me?
All:	Nicked!
Police:	Fixed penalty. £XX:00[3]. *(Exit)*
Andy:	My second… next time I'll be banned!
Jazz:	What'll you do?
Andy:	Be more careful…
Jazz:	Good!
Andy:	Careful not to get nicked again!
Jazz:	Andy… seriously… I don't like it… I don't feel safe!
A:	Let's peek in Andy's mind / to see if we can find some kind / of wisdom… *(Jazz freezes as "A" mimes opening Andy's head… then uses him as a ventriloquists dummy)…* Ah ha! Here we are!
Andy:	*(In a "characterised voice and sits on A's knee as though being operated by "A" as a ventriloquist.)* 50's not fast, 50's not criminal / 50 in a 30 is pretty unexceptional / The police should prioritise use of their time / Murders, rapes, robberies / Solve "proper" crime / Take police off traffic duties they're needed elsewhere / So I can drive fast without pigs in my hair! *(A moves away.)*

---

[3] *Establish what the current fixed penalty is.*

Jazz:	How'll you pay the fine?
Andy:	Grandad sorted it last time. He won't want it to worry my mum.
Jazz:	You don't take it that seriously do you? I'd have to with my dad.
Andy:	Why?
Jazz:	He's a solicitor…
Andy:	Useful!
Jazz:	Don't even go there!
Andy:	I love it when you're angry! *(They strike up a provocative freeze.)*
Both:	Ten weeks on, we're still going strong! *(They repeat the provocative freeze.)*
Jazz:	Half term holiday; Andy springs a surprise!
Andy:	Butlins!
Jazz:	What?
Andy:	Booked a chalet.
Jazz:	One? My dad'll have a fit!
Andy:	Don't tell him!
Jazz:	What if he finds out?
Andy:	He won't.
Jazz:	He could!
Andy:	How?
Jazz:	I don't know… oh you're so…
Andy:	Romantic?
Jazz:	I just wish you'd asked me first.

Section 1

Andy:	I wanted to surprise you!
	(Perhaps some recent summer pop music can provide an atmosphere in the background for the "Butlins sequence" until "Bereavement" when the action stops suddenly. This sequence should be very lively.)
Andy & Jazz:	Butlins! Bargain break!
Jazz:	Bognor!
Andy & Jazz:	*(Both enjoy.)* Bingo and Bowling. *(Jazz enjoys, Andy is bored by:)* Betting at the bookies.
A:	*(Enters taking the bear to Andy.)* Bernie the Bear for…
Andy:	*(Self adoringly.)* Best looking bloke… *(Jazz pretends to be sick)*
Andy & Jazz:	*(Both enjoy.)* Barrels of beer and bopping to bygone bands in the bar.
A:	Bereavement.
Andy:	What? *(Silence)*
Jazz:	Your Grandad's in hospital…
A:	Some kids broke in, he disturbed them.
Jazz:	Seems like he's in a bad way Andy.
A:	Holiday curtailed they dash back home to Surrey. How relevant are speed limits to someone in a hurry? *(Becoming pastiche sports commentator… Murray Walker… with appropriate fx?)* Well good afternoon from the A 24 where Andy Bowen, looking more determined than ever, is already surging ahead. Over the cross roads

without looking, through the chicane, and on to the motorway intersection, and straight into the fast lane! He must be doing well over a hundred, impressive riding and a very brave ride by his pillion Jazzy Mainah. Bowen speeds through the town centre and straight into the hospital car park. Oh my goodness there's an ambulance right in his path, but he's up on a ramp and right over the top of it! What a barnstorming grandstand finish! He richly deserves everything that's coming to him after that ride! Now, lets go live to the hospital waiting area and try to snatch a quick word with what must be… an elated Andy Bowen.

Andy:	*(To Jazz, with a very serious tone.)* We weren't quick enough. He died just before we got here. If we'd stayed at home it wouldn't've happened.
Jazz:	You can't say that.
Andy:	I'd've been there.
Jazz:	Not necessarily…
Andy:	I would. They'd've seen my bike.
Jazz:	You mustn't blame yourself.
A:	An affluent OAP… obvious target, but all they got was twenty quid and a bit of jewellery.
Andy:	He never kept money in the house so what was the point? And after Nan as well…
Jazz:	I loved watching you two together.
Andy:	How can people like that live with themselves?
Jazz:	You couldn't have got here any quicker. You nearly killed us both!
Andy:	Grandad doesn't know that!

Section 1

A: No resolution to that today / So let's speed along the highway of this play / To see bad news turns to good/Like it always should.
(Gives Andy the envelope.)
The inheritance from your Grandad.
For a young lad/such sums can prove dangerous.

Andy: *(Opening the envelope and looks carefully at the enclosed cheque.)* Twenty-five thousand quid.

A: *(As "A" speaks, Andy accompanies the words with appropriate actions/reactions.)* He splashes out on Driving Lessons, and passes first go / With a bucketful of dough / He makes for a local car show / room…

Andy: I want a car that's cool

Salesperson: *(Indicating 'ideal' car)* Anyone ignoring this one, has to be a fool.

Andy: I want a car with power. I want a car for speed.

Salesperson: Look no further… this is the one you need.
Complete with driver's Airbag and ABS brakes, Crash bars and crumple zones for your high speed mistakes.

Andy: I need five spoke alloys, sub-woofer and a CD multi-play!

Salesperson: You can't go wrong with this high performance, top of the range, just look at that spoiler… air conditioned Cabriolet!
Fantastic at the price. You won't find better no matter where you try.
Trust me mate. I'm a car salesman. I wouldn't lie!

Both: *(Shaking hands.)* Deal!

Andy: Done!

Salesperson: You have been! *(Exits)*

Jazz:	*(Entering and getting in the car.)* Smart! Really cool!
Andy:	Wheel spin onto the main road. Speed limit… 30! Speed up to fifty! Speed camera sign… *(under breath)* bollocks! Thirty… nice and innocent. Motorway… test her out! Pratt in the outside lane doing eighty… flash him… drive right up his arse and yeh… he's got the message… flick the V's, overtake and touch on 130 miles per hour… and pose, pose, pose… Some idiot's coming up behind us and isn't slowing down!
Jazz:	Let him pass And.
Andy:	Alright then, but… I could have him!
A:	Slickly Andy switches to the inside lane / and takes a look in the mirror again. Horror of horrors… what does he see?
Andy:	Shit!
Jazz:	What?
Andy:	It's an unmarked police car! He's pulling me over!
Jazz:	You'll be banned!
Andy:	Cheers for the helpful reminder!
Police:	'Ello 'ello 'ello! What's going on here then?
Andy:	Just trying to get out of your way Officer.
Police:	Professional are you?
Andy:	No Officer. *(Aside)*
Jazz:	*(Seductively.)* Recognising that my partner was attempting to maneuver his vehicle out of your, more important path… would you be prepared to… to…?

Section 1

Police:	*(Tapping a hand held device)* I... I... must have been... been mis-reading my... my... but you need to be careful because next time...
Jazz:	Oh... *(Smiling broadly and confidently)*... there's no possibility of there being a "next time" Officer. Is there, Andy?
Andy:	Certainly not!
Police:	Given what a responsible young couple you appear to be I'll issue you with an official warning. *(Exit)*
Andy:	What? *(To Jazz)* He let me off! *(Andy & Jazz look at one another in surprise, clapping hands.)*
Jazz:	Lucky!
Both:	Yeh! Lucky he wasn't a Speed Camera! *(Andy exits.)*
A:	Enough! Let's spice things up, quick change of gears / and re-introduce Kelly MacFarlane, Jazz's friend from nursery years! *(Kelly Enters sullen.)*
Jazz:	I didn't think you were here today.
Kelly:	Zita said you wanted to see me.
Jazz:	You alright?
Kelly:	What did you want?
Jazz:	*(Handing Kelly a slip of paper.)* Look!
Kelly:	Dartington?
Jazz:	My first choice! Doing Drama!
Kelly:	Three B's?
Jazz:	The Bill next...
Kelly:	EastEnders...

Jazz:	Or maybe the RSC.
Kelly:	What?
Jazz:	Royal Shakespeare Company.
Kelly:	Where is Dartington?
Jazz:	Devon. You can come and see me… well us!
Kelly:	What?
Jazz:	Andy's got an offer from Plymouth. A "B" and two "C's".
Kelly:	What if he doesn't get them?
Jazz:	"Piece of piss"… he said. He thought they'd want B's…
Kelly:	He's not doing much work.
Jazz:	He didn't for GCSE's and still got five A*'s and eight A's!
Kelly:	A' Levels are different though… everyone says.
Jazz:	He'll be OK. *(Pause)* Kelly… what's up?
Kelly:	I'm seeing Mr. Minor at one. Dropping out.
Jazz:	What?
Kelly:	Mum and I are… well arguing all the time so I'm moving out too.
Jazz:	Everyone argues.
Kelly:	This is different.
Jazz:	How come?
Kelly:	You don't want to know!
Jazz:	I do!
Kelly:	Promise you won't say anything! Not even to Andy… especially not to Andy.

Section 1

Jazz:	Pregnant?
Kelly:	*(Laughing)* No!
Jazz:	Well what then?
Kelly:	I went to an audition… started off as a joke… but… at a club… for like…
Jazz:	Pole dancing?
Kelly:	Yeh.
Jazz:	Kelly!
Kelly:	Me and Danni got it.
Jazz:	You've told your mum?
Kelly:	Last weekend.
Jazz:	What did she say?
Kelly:	She went ape! What do you think? Be honest.
Jazz:	It's a bit sudden.
Kelly:	It's easy money… and well, I've been dancing since…
Jazz:	Not like that!
Kelly:	But it's easy.
Jazz:	How much do you make?
Kelly:	You pay the club, then what you make, you take home so it depends on how much you do.
Jazz:	Come on then…
Kelly:	Sixty quid!
Jazz:	In one night?
Kelly:	Yeh.

Jazz:	Is it… like full time?
Kelly:	I want to do glamour stuff as well?
Jazz:	Newspapers?
Kelly:	One of the girls there has got this contact… we're going up London… and then, who knows?
Jazz:	I wouldn't have the nerve. *(Andy enters.)*
Kelly:	Don't say anything to Andy… promise!
Andy:	I thought you were off today.
Kelly:	I'm quitting.
Andy:	What school?
Kelly:	Yeh.
Andy:	Why?
Kelly:	It's complicated… anyway I've got to go and see Mr Minor. Well done on your offer.
Andy:	Cheers.
Kelly:	See you.
Jazz:	Tell me how it goes. *(Kelly exits.)*
Andy:	That's weird! Jazz, if I tell you something, you promise not to say anything.
Jazz:	Go on.
Andy:	Dave Weldon says Kelly's been doing dancing… you know… like "dancing"… down at that new Strip Club.
Jazz:	Don't listen to Dave Weldon!
Andy:	Sorree!!! I'm only saying… and then with…
Jazz:	It's just not a very nice thing to say. *(Goes to leave.)*

Section 1

Andy:	I told him it was rubbish… honest!. *(Hesitantly)* Do you want to go to the fair tonight?
Jazz:	I've got an essay due.
Andy:	Everyone else is going!
Jazz:	Go with them then!
Andy:	Is it because of what I just said?
Jazz:	I've just got to do this essay… for Friday.
Andy:	No-one'll bother if it's late.
Jazz:	I want to pass my exams Andy! You seem to do your college work, have a job, and have loads of free time. It's not like that for me. Life's not a "piece of piss"! *(Pause)* We'll go out at the weekend… *(pointedly)*… when you finish work… if you want to go to the fair tonight, go with your mates. I'm off home… I can concentrate there!
Andy:	Do you want a lift?
Jazz:	I'll walk.
Andy:	It's raining?
Jazz:	I like the rain!
Andy:	Liar!
Jazz:	Alright… alright… I'll have a lift if…
Andy:	Yes?
Jazz:	*(Bringing out a CD from her bag.)* If you'll play this!
Andy:	What is it?
Jazz:	*(It could actually be anything… that gets a laugh.[4])* I want you to sing along.

---

[4] *At the time if writing G4's version of Bohemian Rhapsody would seem a possible option.*

Andy:	No problem! *(The chosen song is played with Andy singing heartily… dancing with Jazz. Aim to liven things up and raise a smile!)*
A:	Part 3: A' Level results: *(Giving an envelope to each of them. They walk to opposite sides of the stage and open them.)*
Jazz:	*(Running over to him.)* Andy!
Andy:	What?
Jazz:	A and two B's!
Andy:	*(Trying hard to be pleased for her.)* What did your dad say?
Jazz:	He's paying for driving lessons!
Andy:	You said you didn't want them.
Jazz:	I didn't want you teaching me!
Andy:	Why? Frightened of picking up bad habits?
Jazz:	Frightened I wouldn't pick up any good ones! What about your results?
Andy:	Not so good.
Jazz:	What?
Andy:	*(He shows her the slip of paper.)* A in Computer Studies, E in Maths and N in Chemistry.
Jazz:	You might get in through clearing, won't you?
Andy:	Don't know if I want to anymore.
Jazz:	What'll you do?
Andy:	Stripping?
Jazz:	Who'd pay to see you!

Section 1

Andy:	Dave reckons he can sort an interview with this guy selling advertising space on the Net. I'd get a company car and have the Cabriolet, for weekends. I could get somewhere to rent. Cool eh?
Jazz:	You haven't even got this job yet.
Andy:	Piece of piss! The only thing that bothers me is you going off to Devon and me being stuck up here with nothing to do.
A:	Part 4: Farewell my Lovely. "Good-bye" or "Au-revoir"? The soppy bit! *(Emotional slow dance music begins.)*
Andy:	I'm frightened I'll lose you!
Jazz:	Why?
Andy:	It's obvious.
Jazz:	You've got just as much chance of…
Andy:	Yeh, but I don't want to.
Jazz:	And I do?
Andy:	*(Andy shrugs his shoulders.)* The last year and a half 's been so cool.
A:	*(A walks over to Andy and gives him a sports bag.)* Absence makes the heart grow fonder, and all that stuff?
Andy:	Jazz. *(He puts his hand inside the sports bag.)* I've got something for you. *(He brings out Bernie the Bear.)*
Jazz:	Andy. *(Looking at it.)* He's…
Andy:	I thought he'd remind you of me.
Jazz:	*(Holding it out to examine it.)* I know what you mean! *(They laugh.)*

Andy:	I won him at Bognor, remember?
Jazz:	Yeh… best looking bloke! He's gorgeous *(Hugs the teddy bear close to her.)*
A:	A few tearstained moments later and *(Singing as they part with Jazz waving the Bernie's arm)* Andy and Teddy are waving good-bye.

Section 2: Apart

Kelly:	*(Picking up the phone facing away from Jazz to give the illusion of distance.)* Hi.
Jazz:	*(Speaking into a mobile looking away from Kelly.)* Kells… it's me…
Kelly:	How's it going?
Jazz:	Amazing! You?
Kelly:	I just found myself a bloke.
Jazz:	Me too.
Kelly:	You're joking! What about Andy?
Jazz:	Tell me about yours first.
Kelly:	Tall dark, handsome and… actually it's not as good as it sounds… he's forty-two!
Jazz:	Shit Kelly!
Kelly:	I can't say anymore now…
Jazz:	Come on Kell.
Kelly:	Seriously. When you're back home. What about you? Would I fancy him?
Jazz:	He's a footballer.
Kelly:	Has he got a mate?
Jazz:	He only plays for Torquay…
Kelly:	I bet he's got good legs! And Andy?
Jazz:	I'll probably chuck him… but don't say anything Kell, please.
Kelly:	I never see him… how did you meet this footballer?
Jazz:	In the Student Union Bar… *(As she describes their meeting they come together as though in the bar. Possibly pre-recorded music fades up. Jazz puts*

the mobile away as the scene merges.) He was going out with this girl from our Hall… and… well you know… we got talking!

Matt: *(Laughing)* Go on then!

Jazz: Why?

Matt: Just do it!.

Jazz: It's a trick!

Matt: Lick your palm!

Jazz: *(Jazz licks her palm.)* Now what?

Matt: Did it taste of salt?

Jazz: No.

Matt: That's all right then.

Jazz: What do you mean?

Matt: If it tastes of salt it means you'll die at sea. I heard it on the radio.

Jazz: *(Laughing)* You're mad you are!

(Andy is sat on the other side of the stage. The action from this point on switches between Andy and Jazz/Matt)

Andy: *(Writing or reading through his email.)* Jazz, hope you're getting on OK and haven't met too many blokes you fancy. It'll be brilliant when you come and stay. I've found a bedsit. The people who were here before got chucked out 'cos it was in a tip. I cleared it up for a discount on the first month's rent. The loo was disgusting with crap up the wall! *(Continues to type/read [silently] as the scene continues.)*

Matt: *(Jazz and Matt are laughing together.)* The secret is to breathe in as you do it… like this. *(Matt impersonates a dog barking.)* Go on!

Section 2

Jazz:	Are all footballers mad?
Matt:	Whenever I score the whole crowd barks. It's funny! If you come you've got to learn to do it.
Jazz:	*(She clears her throat and makes an attempt at it. It makes her cough.)* I can't!
Matt:	By Christmas you'll be howling for me!
Andy:	Bumped into Kelly yesterday. Have you heard? Some bloke at her club started pestering her and she ended up with the club saying she was a prostitute and sacking her! She's moving back in with her mum and getting a moped with the money she made. I told her to get a Harley... she said she didn't have enough!
Jazz:	*(Jazz and Matt are speaking quietly and intimately.)* When did it happen?
Matt:	Last year.
Jazz:	I'm sorry...
Matt:	No, talking about him's good. Best way to keep him real. The bloke who ran into him was a known druggie... always drove like that... but no-one ever did anything... Iain and me wanted to go round and sort him out but we never did. We felt so useless.
Jazz:	What happened?
Matt:	He got six months... but probably got more gear there than outside, and when he comes out he'll just do it again? I don't know how people like that live with themselves?
Jazz:	They just blank it out... I guess.
Matt:	Iain and me still put flowers on the verge where he was killed.

Jazz:	How old was he?
Matt:	Frankie?
Jazz:	Yeh.
Matt:	He was my twin.
Andy:	The cars at the garage being fixed cos I had a little shunt yesterday. I'll be coming up by train so won't be there until 1:06 in the morning! I'm alright and it wasn't my fault… well… not completely!
Jazz:	*(Jazz, is reading on a screen or phone.)* Really looking forward to seeing you. Love ya, And.
Matt:	*(Entering)* Who's that from?
Jazz:	A friend.
Matt:	No-one special then?
Jazz:	It's my boyfriend… from home.
Matt:	Why haven't you said before?
Jazz:	He's coming up on Friday so I would have told you. I'm gonna chuck him… but not till Sunday.
Matt:	Why don't you tell him on the phone?
Jazz:	He deserves more than that… but Matt, I want to be with you. *(She hugs him.)*
A:	*(Andy enters carrying a sports bag and studying some directions.)* Somewhere near Yellow House on Friday night Andy's lost…
Andy:	*(Angrily)*… Jazz's map is Shiite!
A:	Then walking towards him, a figure he can see
Andy:	*(To Matt.)* Oy. Excuse-us. Please… can you help me?

Section 2

A:	What a coincidence!
Matt:	What is it mate?
Andy:	Is this Yellow House?
Matt:	Yeh.
Andy:	I'm looking for Room 102.
Matt:	102? Jazzy Mainah?
Andy:	Yeh.
Matt:	There's a guy on duty by the lift. He'll let you in, well if she's expecting you.
Andy:	I'm her boyfriend.
Matt:	You?
Andy:	Yeh. Why?
Matt:	Lucky bloke you are. I know her! When you see her, tell her Barking Matt said hello. *(Exits barking.)*
Jazz:	*(Enters.)* He doesn't even go to the College.
Andy:	Why was he here then?
Jazz:	He's got a girlfriend in the next door hall.
Andy:	What does he do?
Jazz:	He's a footballer.
Andy:	Professional?
Jazz:	Think so.
Andy:	Who does he play for?
Jazz:	Torquay. What's with all the questions?
Andy:	As in Torquay United? They were talking about him on the telly the other day.
Jazz:	You don't even like football!

Andy:	I was round at Dave's. They all bark at him. He scored and the commentators were saying about it. Bloody show off… he even barked as he walked away from me.
Jazz:	Can we change the subject now?
Andy:	I reckon he fancies you!
Jazz:	Andy, if you're going to be like this all the time… well it's not going to be much of a weekend is it?
A:	*(As though a football commentator, an imitation would be ideal.)* Just the warning yellow card this time… but with Irvine constantly hanging around the box, Bowen needs to be careful. But look out on yonder penalty area. *(Matt enters… all in slow motion. It is essential that Jazz and Matt are choreographed appropriately to indicate the meaning of the words.)* Irvine's placing the ball on the spot. A short run up and… yes he's scored! What a goal! Listen to that crowd barking like rabid dogs! Football certainly is a funny old game and Irvine seems likely to consign out of form Bowen to the inevitable free transfer.
Matt:	*(To audience)*… if anyone will have him. You'll never guess what?
Jazz:	What?
Matt:	*(Laughing)* I met your boyfriend.
Jazz:	He said.
Matt:	*(Laughing)* He asked me for directions. Me?
Jazz:	I know.
Matt:	So? You told him?
Jazz:	I'm seeing him next week-end at home and…
Matt:	I told Carrie… you promised!

Section 2

Jazz:	I felt too guilty what with him coming up all this way and…
Matt:	What about me?
Jazz:	What do you mean?
Matt:	You sounded so sure before.
Jazz:	Matt… I will. Trust me.
Matt:	What… like he does?
Andy:	*(Jazz & Matt kiss and talk closely throughout Andy's letter.)* Dear Jazz, when I got back home yesterday night I sat in my bath looking at the photos of us at Bognor and cried for ages. I'm seriously thinking of packing my job in and coming down to be with you. What do you think?
A:	On and on the letter goes / in Andy's rather soppy prose/a fresh one in the post each day / *(Jazz is given a bouquet. Matt is not impressed and turns away)* / and then a very posh bouquet.
Jazz:	*(To Matt)* I didn't ask him to send the bloody thing!

Section 3: Fatality

A:	Wednesday afternoon, Andy's in a flurry / Hurrying to an appointment / Can't rub ointment/on the fact he's late / which only serves to vindicate /to him, his gratuitous greed / for speed.
Andy:	*(Spoken hurriedly, anxiously, as though "against the clock")* If I can do a journey in twenty minutes, I'll only give it twenty minutes, it's stupid, 'cos work are very strict on time keeping.
A:	Andy's created a custom built cause to go quick / after all, speeding's only "speeding" if you're doing it for a kick / the ingredients laid out before you, ready to inflict / the R.T.A. so easy to predict / and so simple to avoid.
	(Loud music plays. Cathy is off stage. Kelly is putting on coat, shoes and rucksack ready to go out.)
Kelly:	Mum!
Cathy:	*(Off)* What?
Kelly:	Can you lend me a fiver… petrol for moped. Interview at the supermarket. Remember?
Cathy:	*(Off)* Forgot… sorry.
Kelly:	Pay you back when I get my job!
Cathy:	*(Entering and getting the money from her wallet.)* What if you don't?
Kelly:	He already said he liked the look of me!
Cathy:	You watch him. *(She gives Kelly the money.)*
Kelly:	Thanks Mum. *(Kisses her. Picks up [from A] a cheap and much used motorcycle helmet.)* I'll be back as soon as I can… just after five I guess. *(Kelly freezes.)*
Cathy:	*(Momentary pause.)* Good luck Kelly. *(Freeze)*

Section 3

(Silence.)

You never know when you're seeing someone for the last time. Perhaps that's for the best, but I look back and I wish I'd made that moment special:

Kelly: Mum! Can you lend me a fiver... petrol for my moped. Interview at the supermarket. Remember?

Cathy: *(Getting a twenty pound not from wallet.)* There you are sweetheart. Get yourself something with the change...

Kelly: Twenty pounds? Hey... thanks... why?

Cathy: If you get the job, a kind of congratulations... and if not... well... you know...

Kelly: *(Confused)* Thanks Mum! *(They Hug.)*

Cathy: Kell, I'm so relieved you're back home.

Kelly: It was all stupid.

Cathy: I love you Kell. More than you can possibly know... I had no idea how much I could love someone until you came along.

Kelly: What's brought all this on?

Cathy: Just wanted you to know.

Kelly: You're not so bad yourself. *(Kisses her. Starts to put on the motorcycle helmet she already has.)* Look, I'll be back as soon as I can... just after five I guess. *(Kelly freezes.)*

Cathy: We'll have a take away tonight eh? Chinese?

Kelly: Yeh! See you mum! *(Exits)*

Cathy: But that couldn't change the fact that Kelly wouldn't come back... that's what I can't get over... there's nothing I could do... but this guy who killed her... there was so much he could have done… so much… but he didn't… I don't know how he lives with himself.

A: *(Looking at, or touching Kelly.)* Disposing of someone by crashing into them is easy…

Andy: *(To audience)* It's a great day for driving… perfect weather, I reckon I can make up some time so set myself a challenge: "How fast dare I go?" Speed helps me focus my mind, I concentrate better and I'm more careful. There's a bend coming up, round to the left, wide with verges on both sides sweeping out into a straight, *(laughing)* I take it at about 60, the car on the edge of control…
the power!

A: Isn't there a school on one side?

Andy: *(To A, snapping out of the previous speech)* My old one, but they finished about an hour ago… it's all fenced off this side, so it's not a problem. *(In slow motion, with the fx. as used in Section 1 Andy comes back into the scene, speaking to audience. He starts speaking once his "driving" position has been reassumed.)* I'm on the straight now and decelerating cos there's a sharper bend coming up. I guess I'm doing about 50…

A: *(To Audience.)* More like 60.

Andy: *(To A, again snapping out of the previous speech)* Everyone breaks the speed limit here!

A: Everyone?

Andy: Take the 40 sign away, you'd guess it's derestricted. Anyway they'd have cameras there if they thought it was a problem.

A: Carry on.

Andy: I'm on the straight now, doing 70, no longer feeling as if I'm going "fast".

Section 3

A:	*(Standing to the left of Andy)* Garage forecourt.
Kelly:	*(Kelly, surrounded by three threatening individuals, B, C, & D)* Girl on moped.
A:	Excellent visibility.
All (Except Andy):	Throttle!
Andy:	She's not looking!
All (Except Andy):	Throttle!
All:	Stop!!! *(Kelly & A-D say this to Andy. Andy to Kelly. "A" simultaneously attempts to reach out to prevent Andy from hitting Kelly. They could attempt to "stop" Kelly. It is important in the following moments that the elements of the crash are explored physically as the words are spoken. The violence of the death, and the pain he repeatedly and without mercy, inflicts on her should be highlighted in the physicalisation. The violence of the accident should be conveyed over and above these instructions to being followed blindly. The director should use slow motion allowing physical contact to be made without physical injury being caused and also allowing the audience to scrutinise the reactions of all those involved in greater detail. Andy should actually be seen to be hurting Kelly and her reactions should be visible. He should beat her with either with fists or metal bars every time she is "hit" in the accident after the initial impact. He should put great physical effort into the "killing". The "blows" in the written script are for guidance only. Some may be single blows, some may be a rally of blows.)*
D:	Sound the horn!
C:	Slam on brakes.
All (Except Andy):	Wheels lock… Skid!

B: *(The witness):* Car… opposite direction… swerves.

All: *(As Andy makes his first violent – slow motion – contact with Kelly)* No!!!

B: *(2nd blow.)* Her body smashes the windscreen.

D: Rolls over the roof…

B: Down the back panel.

C: Onto the grass verge.

All (Except Andy): *(Andy throws his final blow. Kelly is lowered into her "resting" position by A-D simulating her final slow motion fall.)* Into a lamp post.

(Silence)

Andy: I come to a halt on the grass verge. Glass everywhere. *(Re-living the crash)* The rider turned towards me after she started across the road… she hadn't looked before. I was convinced she'd stop or slow so… so I swerved to the right to avoid her. *(Pause)*
I hit her bike on the right hand side of the road.
I get out of the car and see a mangled body slumped by the lamp-post. People come over from the houses:

Neighbour 1: *(Attending to Kelly)* Get an ambulance… quick!

Neighbour 2: Anyone know First Aid?

Andy: She didn't look…

Neighbour 2: Come on mate.

Andy: She just flew out of the garage.

Neighbour 2: Your face is cut.

Andy: It's nothing serious.

Neighbour 2: *(Moving Andy away from Kelly.)* You come over here, wait for the ambulance.

Section 3

Andy:	*(To Audience.)* I saw the bone in her leg sticking out, like raw meat on a butcher's table. *(Grabbing and addressing Neighbour 2.)* Tell me there was nothing I could do! Tell me she didn't look! *(Pause)* Tell me you don't think I was going too fast!
Neighbour 2:	*(Trying to calm Andy.)* No-one's doubting you mate and the woman in that car must have seen what happened.
Andy:	Yeh… *(Slowly)*… she must have done. *(To audience)* The police and the ambulance arrived after about 7 or 8 minutes I suppose.
Paramedic 1:	*(Entering)* Look at those skids.
Paramedic 2:	He must have been doing some.
Paramedic 1:	Smashed the helmet… look!
Paramedic 2:	A cheap one.
Paramedic 1:	Ankle torn away…
Paramedic 2:	… and the two bones below her knee are out. *(Paramedic 3 goes to Andy.)*
Paramedic 1:	Blood from the ear and nose… suspect a severe injury to the base of her skull… or depressed fractures. *(They continue the examination and carefully load Kelly onto a stretcher and take her off during the following dialogue.)*
Paramedic 3:	What's your name?
Andy:	Andy. Andy Bowen.
Paramedic 3:	Right Andy. I've come to see how you are. Do you think you've got any injuries?
Andy:	Don't you think you'd be more use over there?
Paramedic 3:	We've got to check you over, and the police'll have to breathalyse you.

Andy: The girl... will she die?

Paramedic 3: They'll do all they can for her.

Andy: What if she does?

Paramedic 3: You can't think like that.

Andy: She didn't look before she pulled out. I didn't mean to...
(Pause)
Then I heard it... just what I didn't want to hear... the only person who'd witnessed the accident ranting:

Witness: She didn't stand a chance! He's a bloody maniac! She didn't stand a chance poor love.

A: And that "poor love" a family she had / hearing such news was painfully bad / her mother still doesn't speak much of it to this day / but here's a little of what she does choose to say:

Cathy: Once the moped started across the road he appears... 100 metres away. Traveling at over seventy in a forty.

Andy: *(To audience)* I tell the police that I was driving within the speed limit. What else could I say?

Cathy: He gave my Kelly one and a half seconds to turn back.

Andy: She didn't look! There was nothing I could do!

Cathy: Then they allowed him to go home! Kelly was lying there, in the mortuary! I thought that they'd sort him out but what did they do... allowed him to go home!
(B, C, D & Kelly leave inconspicuously.)

Andy: I phone a couple of people and have a few drinks. I imagine the doorstep scene for her parents and I

Section 3

feel guilty... I imagine them crying at her bedside... this poor mangled kid. I ring the hospital and enquire about how she is, but they won't tell me anything. Then finally really late at night... the phone rings:

D.I. Morris: Is that Mr. Andrew Bowen?

Andy: Yes.

Cathy: What's happened?

D.I. Morris: This is DI Morris. I'm afraid I've got very bad news regarding your accident yesterday afternoon.

Andy: She's died hasn't she?

Cathy: No... killed! Seventy in a forty! What chance did she stand?

D.I. Morris: Do you have a solicitor?

Cathy: *(To Andy)* Let the courts deal with it? What can they do? Our friends'll sort him out! We'll make him realise what he's done! I know I shouldn't say this, but I'd like to kill him. I hate thinking like this, but I can't help it. He's just got to pay!

Andy: Can you tell me her name?

D.I. Morris: Do you think it would help?

Andy: I'd like to know.

D.I. Morris: Kelly... Kelly MacFarlane.

Cathy: I've just thought... her room? What am I going to do with her room... the CD she was playing before she left for that interview. What shall I do with her room?

Andy: How old was she?

D.I. Morris: Eighteen.

Andy:	But I know her… bloody hell… Kelly MacFarlane who lives in Park Road?
D.I. Morris:	Yes.
Andy:	I went to school with her… she's one of my girlfriends mates. It can't be. *(He puts the phone down.)* Why the fuck didn't she look before she pulled out?

Section 4: Outcast

(Andy, carrying sports bag in one hand, arrives in Jazz's room where a tape plays quietly throughout scene.)

A:	Both Andy and Jazz have facts to reveal before the end / he to explain how he killed her best friend / she to tell him that their bubble's now burst / what words will they summon, and who, Andy or Jazz, will dare to tell first?
Andy:	Am I glad to see you? *(Goes to hug her)*
Jazz:	*(Holding him at arms length and looking at his cut face.)* You're cut?
Andy:	I know.
Jazz:	Been in a fight?
Andy:	Not yet.
Jazz:	What do you mean?
Andy:	*(Moving away from her, goes down on his knees to unzip his bag and takes out a bottle of wine.)* Got a corkscrew?
Jazz:	I don't know. *(Starts to look half-heartedly, for a corkscrew.)* Actually Andy, *(Takes the wine and puts it back in Andy's bag)* I don't want to drink and I don't really think you should either.
Andy:	What?
Jazz:	When you phoned this afternoon I dropped my plans for tonight…
Andy:	What?
Jazz:	I've got a life here Andy!
Andy:	That makes me feel a whole lot better… cos me… I'm in trouble, real trouble. *(Jazz's mobile rings. She goes to pick it up.)*
Jazz:	*(She stops the call.)* I'll get it later…

Andy:	No… take it… don't mind me… you've got your life to lead!
Jazz:	I want you to tell me what's happened, it's only Kell. *(Pause)*
Andy:	Who?
Jazz:	Kelly… MacFarlane?
Andy:	Can't be!
Jazz:	Look! *(Shows the phone to him.)*
Andy:	Someone's got her phone then.
Jazz:	I'll call her back.
Andy:	Don't! She… Jazz, that's why I'm here.
Jazz:	What are you on about?
Andy:	It's really bad news Jazz.
Jazz:	What do you mean?
Andy:	She's been killed…. on her moped…
Jazz:	Kelly?
Andy:	Yesterday.
Jazz:	Who was that on the phone then?
Andy:	I don't know.
Jazz:	I'll call her back…
Andy:	No, don't! Please Jazz… don't…
Jazz:	Why not?
Andy:	Just don't alright!
Jazz:	Why? Why are you being like this?
Andy:	Please listen to what I've got to say.

Section 4

Jazz:	I want to speak to… whoever's got her phone… I want to know what's happened! I want to know what's going on!
Andy:	What're you going to do when you've found out?
Jazz:	I don't know… but I've got to do something… she's my mate Andy! *(Pause)* It's so unfair 'cos she was really starting to sort her life out. When did you hear about it? *(Silence)*
Andy:	I was there. *(Silence)*
Jazz:	What?
Andy:	It was me… that's what I've come to tell you.
Jazz:	No!
Andy:	She pulled out without looking. I didn't know it was Kelly till last night. I'm so sorry Jazz. *(Silence)*
Jazz:	When did it happen?
Andy:	Yesterday… afternoon…
Jazz:	Where?
Andy:	Vattingstone Lane.
Jazz:	Behind our old school?
Andy:	*(Nods in agreement.)* She just pulled out of the garage without looking! *(Message alert tone sounds… Andy grabs the mobile, but Jazz managers to keep it.)*
Jazz:	What're you doing? *(She calling the answering service.)* It's Kelly's number again… voicemail.
Andy:	Listen Jazz.

Jazz:	No! I want to hear this message! *(Silence)* It's Kelly's mum. *(For the first time on the edge of tears)* I can't believe this. Do they know it was you?
Andy:	Look… I need you to hear this from me. They're saying I was speeding.
Jazz:	Were you?
Andy:	I didn't think so.
Jazz:	Who says you were then?
Andy:	Accident Investigation Unit.
Jazz:	Were you or weren't you? Why are they saying it? How do they know?
Andy:	They did these tests. I had to sit and watch. They drive along the road at forty, and then brake where my skids began. They keep doing it… going faster and faster until finally the car reaches the point where I hit the…
Jazz:	How fast?
Andy:	You don't want to know.
Jazz:	Tell me Andy!
Andy:	They're saying seventy… but I'm sure I wasn't… I
Jazz:	You must have been! *(More detached)* Andy? How did you get here?
Andy:	What?
Jazz:	Tell me you came by train.
Andy:	No.
Jazz:	You drove?
Andy:	Can't you be more understanding?

Section 4

Jazz:	You killed my mate and you want me to be "more understanding"? *(Silence)* Remember how you felt when your Grandad died. You wanted those kids locked up! You wanted the key thrown away. I can hear you say it!
Andy:	They were robbing him! They were breaking the law!
Jazz:	So were you!
Andy:	They'd done it before.
Jazz:	So had you! Loads of times!
Andy:	Jazz, please…
Jazz:	I want you to go!
Andy:	I need you to help me.
Jazz:	I can't. Not now
Andy:	You've got to.
Jazz:	I can't look at you without thinking what you've done… we're finished Andy.
Andy:	Don't say that Jazz.
Jazz:	She was my mate! *(Silence)*
Andy:	Please Jazz!
Jazz:	There's nothing more to say.
Andy:	Look, I'll go but let me come back in an hour or so when you've had time to…
Jazz:	I don't want to see you again… not ever. I mean it!
Andy:	*(Laughs nervously.)* You don't! You can't!
Jazz:	I do. I want you to go.

Andy:	You're all I've got… there must be something I can do!
Jazz:	Bring Kelly back!
Andy:	That's a shit thing to say.
Jazz:	Andy just go! *(Silence)*
Andy:	Let me give you a hug. Please! We both need one. *(Andy holds out his arms. Both he and Jazz are motionless for a moment or two.)*
Jazz:	OK… but…
Andy:	*(Approaching her)* Please Jazz… don't say any more. *(They hug, she somewhat hesitantly. The silence is broken by Matt "barking" repeatedly – and loudly – off stage.)*
Jazz:	*(Under her breath)* Shit!
Andy:	What?
Jazz:	I don't believe it! *(Matt Enters. Jazz and Andy part.)*
Matt:	*(To Jazz)* This explains why you weren't at the match!
Andy:	What are you doing here?
Jazz:	Something's happened. I left a message on your mobile.
Matt:	Forgot it. Didn't think you'd stand me up!
Andy:	Am I hearing this right?
Matt:	*(To Jazz)* My mates wanted to meet you.
Jazz:	Matt, not now!
Andy:	*(Turning Jazz round.)* What's going on?

Section 4

Matt:	*(Pulling Andy away.)* Don't you dare touch her mate!
Andy:	*(To Matt)* You on the wind up? *(Andy confronts Matt.)*
Matt:	Go on mate… take a pop at me?
Andy:	Don't tempt me!
Jazz:	Leave it Matt!
Matt:	Come on then! It'll go down a storm in the tabloids! "Two Goal Cup Hero, Irvine… Beaten up in College Brawl".
Jazz:	Stop it Matt!
Andy:	You promised me last week everything was OK.
Jazz:	*(Shouting!)* Matt, Andy's been involved in a serious accident.
Matt:	He seems alright.
Jazz:	Well I'm not! He killed one of my best mates! *(She breaks down.)* *(Silence)*
Matt:	You what?
Andy:	She was a learner… on a moped.
Jazz:	You were driving too fast, you always go too fucking fast!
Andy:	Thanks Jazz.
Matt:	*(To Andy)* Mate, I lost my twin brother because of some maniac driver!
Andy:	What's that to do with me?
Matt:	*(Approaching and grabbing Andy overpowering him.)* Everything!

Jazz:	Leave him Matt!
Andy:	Fucking let go!
Matt:	*(Still maintaining control.)* You put your foot on the accelerator... didn't you? no-one made you! *(He throws Andy away from him.)*
Andy:	You can't stand in judgment over me... not after what you've done!
Matt:	What?
Andy:	Getting in with my girlfriend... you're out of order...
Matt:	It's not in the same league as killing someone mate.
Jazz:	Go Andy! Just go, please, before this all gets out of hand!
Andy:	He wouldn't dare do anything!
Matt:	I wouldn't bet on it!
Jazz:	Andy... just go!
Matt:	Do you want me to make you mate... 'cos I will!
Andy:	*(To Jazz.)* I don't believe you... I thought...
Jazz:	*(Screaming)* Get out! *(Andy exits)* *(Jazz turns to Matt, tearful. They hug.)*
A:	And so / on that sour note Jazz and Andy go / each their separate way / But this play / is not done / till one year on / Crown Court judgment day.
	"Human blood is heavy; the man that has shed it cannot run away."
	A verdict of "Guilty!" is quickly returned / our "hero" feels spurned / they strip away his freedom... tear away his pride / he's given...

Section 4

All:	… eighteen months…
A:	… banged up inside.
All:	And a five year driving ban. *(Silence. Everyone exits leaving Andy alone on stage.)*
Andy:	The shock and distress of killing someone is immense, I wouldn't want to understate that at all… but the shock and life upset of going to prison has for me been even greater. It's a sad fact but it is true. So, if someone pulls out in front of you and you happen to be over the speed limit… you end up in prison. Just be aware of that.
	And Jazz? She was in the national newspaper last week… arm in arm with barking Matt Irvine, now playing in the Premier League. She jacked Uni in for him… and they're having difficulties apparently. Although they both deny it! Difficulties them? Whatever they're going through is a piece of piss compared to being in prison! It's a nightmare… I tell you it's totally screwed me up!
Prisoner 1:	So, it was you who killed that eighteen year old kid?
Andy:	It was a car accident.
Prisoner 2:	You're smiling!
Prisoner 1:	Laughing about it.
Prisoner 2:	You're not taking it very seriously!
Prisoner 1:	You didn't even have the bottle to plead guilty.
Andy:	It wasn't all my fault.
Prisoner 1:	You're not listening!
Prisoner 2:	You're not even sorry!
Prisoner 1:	You killed a kid.

Andy:	Let me explain!
Prisoner 1 & 2:	What is there to explain?
Andy:	These massive blokes just burst into my cell behind them and one brought out a jug from behind his back, full of boiling water, and hurled it at me… in my face… everywhere, then ran out, banging the cell door locked behind them.
	The boiling water was laced with sugar… so it stuck to my skin… lethal! Fortunately I had a sink, so I put the plug in, switched on the cold water, and plunged my face straight in. Although that helped I couldn't stop it soaking through my sweatshirt and leaving painful red marks on my chest that'll serve as a reminder for the rest of my life.
	(In slow motion Prisoners each hurl the contents of a [mimed] jug at Andy, who screams a prolonged scream. The style of the final moment of action should reflect elements of the staging of the accident scene in Section 3, i.e. "an eye for an eye". The lights cross fade and remain on the slogan at the back of the stage.)

Other plays published by *dbda*

If you have enjoyed reading and/or working with this playscript, you may like to find out about other plays we publish. There are brief descriptions and other details on the following pages.

All plays deal with contemporary social and moral issues and are suitable for Youth Theatres, Schools, Colleges, and adult AmDram. They are ideal for GCSE Drama/English exam use and frequently do well in One Act Play Festivals. They offer both male and female performers equally challenging opportunities.

For enquiries or to order plays published by *dbda*, please contact:
dbda, Pin Point, Rosslyn Crescent, Harrow HA1 2SB.
Tel: 0870 333 7771
Fax: 0870 333 7772
Email: info@dbda.co.uk

All enquiries regarding performing rights of plays by
***Mark Wheeller*, should be made to:**
Sophie Gorel Barnes, MBA Literary Agents,
62 Grafton Way, London W1P 5LD.
Tel: 020 7387 2076
Email: sophie@mbalit.co.uk

All enquiries regarding performing rights of 'Heroin Lies'
by *Wayne Denfhy*, should be made to:
Wayne Denfhy, c/o *dbda*,
Pin Point, Rosslyn Crescent, Harrow HA1 2SB.
Tel: 0870 333 7771
Email: info@dbda.co.uk (subject: Wayne Denfhy)

All enquiries regarding performing rights of 'Gagging For It'
by *Danny Sturrock*, should be made to:
Danny Sturrock, c/o *dbda*,
Pin Point, Rosslyn Crescent, Harrow HA1 2SB.
Tel: 0870 333 7771
Email: info@dbda.co.uk (subject: Danny Sturrock)

Other plays published by *dbda*

ISBN 1 902843 17 1

Cast: 3f, 3m &3m/f or 3m & 3f for GCSE using suggested cuts
Duration: 55 minutes approx.
KS 3 & 4

NEW – Gagging for it by Danny Sturrock

Summer is here, A-levels are over and a group of 6 friends embark on a holiday to Ibiza! What would their holiday bring? Would Chris finally pluck up the courage to ask out Teresa? Would Jay drink himself into oblivion? Would Bianca spend the entire holiday flirting with the Spanish barmen – more than likely! ...or would a chance encounter with an old friend bring their hedonistic worlds crashing down around them!?

Comedy, dance music and choreography are the keys to this production. The pace is breakneck and hilarious, but once the party's over, it hits you!

'Really funny... laugh out loud funny. Inspired outstanding performances from the six Year 11s who went on to exceed our expectations by a long way in their GCSEs achieving A or A*. It proved to be a firm favourite with our KS3/4 audience.'

Mark Wheeller

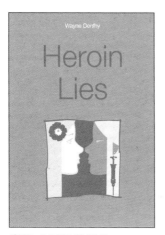

ISBN 1 902843 15 0

Cast: 8f, 7m and 2m/f
Duration: 70 minutes approx.
KS 3 & 4

Heroin Lies by Wayne Denfhy

A sensitive, yet disturbing look at drugs and drug dependency, in particular the pressures and influences at play on an ordinary teenage girl. We observe Vicki's gradual and tragic slide towards addiction and also the various degrees of help and hindrance she receives from family and friends.

This is a new, updated edition of Wayne Denfhy's popular play. It is suitable for performance as well as for reading in the class. Included with the playscript is an excellent scheme for follow-up work by Peter Rowlands.

'...a piece of drama that will stimulate and challenge a young cast... Heroin Lies deals with vital issues that affect today's youngsters in a gentle and humane way and, in so doing, gets its message across without the instant rejection that can meet other approaches.'

Pete Sanpher, Head of Drama, Norfolk

The Gate Escape by Mark Wheeller

The story of two truants. Corey is 'addicted' to bunking school. Chalkie views himself as a casual truant "no problem!" While truanting with some friends, the pair are greeted by a surreal 'Big Brother' figure who sets them a task. The loser will be in for some dramatic 'Big Bother'... Who will lose?... What will this 'bother' be?

The play has toured professionally throughout the south of England to great acclaim.

'A lively dramatic style and innovative structure with dynamic and contemporary dialogue. It is written in a way to guarantee that the audience will feel fully involved and enthralled by the main characters.'

Professor Ken Reid, Author of Tackling Truancy in Schools

ISBN 1 902843 14 2

Cast: *2f & 2m with doubling, or up to 30*
Duration: *70 minutes approx.*
KS 3 & 4

'Theatrically interesting... excellent basis for active discussion of issues and dramatic style with reluctant GCSE students'

Ali Warren (National Drama)

Too Much Punch for Judy by Mark Wheeller

A hard-hitting documentary play, based on a tragic drink-drive accident that results in the death of Jo, front seat passenger. The driver, her sister Judy, escapes unhurt (or has she?).

The tragic incident was dramatised by Mark in 1986 using only the words of those most closely involved and affected. This play has become one of the most frequently performed plays ever!

'The play will have an impact on young people or adults. It will provoke discussion. It stimulates and wants you to cry out for immediate social action and resolution.'

Henry Shankula – Addiction Research Foundation, Toronto

ISBN 1 902843 05 3

Cast: *2f & 2m with doubling or 3f, 3m & 6*
Duration: *50 minutes approx.*
KS 4 to adult

'The young audience I was sat in was patently out for some whooping Friday night fun... at the end there was a horrid silence.'

Nick Baker – Times Educational Supplement

Other plays published by *dbda*

GRAHAM – World's Fastest Blind Man!
by Mark Wheeller

A play full of lively humour telling the inspirational story of Graham Salmon MBE. Totally blind since birth, Graham went on to become the World's Fastest Blind Man running 100 metres in 11.4 seconds! The play, written in Mark's unique documentary style, skillfully brings to life Graham's courage, tenacity and wonderful sense of humour.

'Very good, very moving, very very funny!'

Bruce Henderson, Principal Teacher of Drama,
Wester Hailes Education Centre, Edinburgh

'I was really wowed by Graham... offered excellent opportunities for imaginative stylised performance with GCSE students... The peaks of tension and moments of pathos really moved me... I will definitely be offering Graham to my classes this year.'

Neil Phillips, Head of Drama and Edexcel GCSE Examiner

ISBN 1 902843 09 6

Cast: 5m & 4f with doubling, or up to 34
Duration: 80 minutes approx.
KS 3/4 to adult

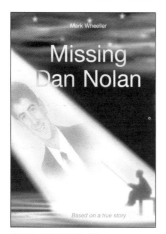

Missing Dan Nolan (based on a true story)
by Mark Wheeller

This play, based on the true story of Dan Nolan, a teenage boy who went missing on the night of January 1st 2002, is written in the same documentary style as 'Too Much Punch for Judy'. During 2003, it has been shown at various Drama Festivals and has won awards and commendations at every one!

'Unusual and deeply affecting. Skillfully written... achieves astonishing depth and authenticity... addresses a wound still raw and stands as a fitting testament to a young life.'

Charles Evans, Adjudicator, Eastleigh Drama Festival

'I feel very proud. All the issues about our Dan's disappearance, and the safety issues surrounding teenagers, are in the play and it will continue to raise awareness'

Pauline Nolan (Dan's mother)

ISBN 1 902843 16 9

Cast: 2m & 2f with doubling, or up to 18
Duration: 45-50 minutes
KS 3/4 to adult

Hard to Swallow by Mark Wheeller

This play is an adaptation of Maureen Dunbar's award winning book (and film) **Catherine** which charts her daughter's uneven battle with anorexia and the family's difficulties in coping with the illness.

The play has gone on to be performed all over the world to much acclaim, achieving considerable success in One Act Play Festivals. Its simple narrative style means that it is equally suitable for adult and older youth groups to perform.

'This play reaches moments of almost unbearable intensity... naturalistic scenes flow seamlessly into sequences of highly stylised theatre... such potent theatre!'

Vera Lustiq, The Independent

'Uncompromising and sensitive... should be compulsory viewing to anyone connected with the education of teenagers.'

Mick Martin, Times Educational Supplement

ISBN 1 902843 08 8

Cast: 3f & 2m with doubling, or 6f, 3m & 16
Duration: 70 minutes
KS 3 to adult

Why did the chicken cross the road? by Mark Wheeller

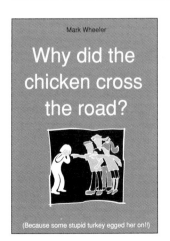

The story of two cousins, Tammy and Chris. Tammy gets killed in a stupid game of 'chicken' on the one morning that the cousins do not cycle to school. Chris, unable to tell anyone else about his part in the accident, has to live with this dreadful secret.

'An imaginative and moving look at risk taking at a time when peer pressure is at its strongest.'

Rosie Welch, LARSOA

'Recommended... conveys important messages through entertainment. Audience were engrossed, looking for reactions and listening intently.'

Craig Taylor, Senior Manager
Ecclesbourne Primary School, Islington

ISBN 1 902843 00 2

Cast: 2m & 2f with doubling, or 3f, 3m & 3
Duration: 35 minutes
KS 3 & 4

Other plays published by *dbda*

Wacky Soap – *a Musical with a difference...*

Wacky Soap is a Pythonesque allegorical tale about 'substance' abuse (drugs, alcohol, glue, tobacco, etc). While washing with Wacky Soap leads to instant happiness and an inclination towards outrageous behaviour, prolonged use washes away limbs and ultimately leads to dematerialisation. This has become a tried and tested (and increasingly popular) School/ Drama Club/Youth Theatre production and is an ideal vehicle for a cast of any age.

The story of Wacky Soap, by Mark Wheeller, first appeared as a full **Musical play.** The play script of the full version (shown below) includes scheme of work for KS3/4. A mini version of the play is included with the **Music Score.**

ISBN 1 902843 02 9
KS 3/4 to adult

Wacky Soap – A Cautionary Tale by Mark Wheeller

Cast: 6-100!

Duration: 50 mins play / 80 mins musical

'This (play) gave every member of the large and energetic cast opportunities to shine... King Huff addressed his subjects from a Bouncy Castle, just one of the touches of visual humour in this fast, funny and thought provoking evening'.

Barbara Hart, Southern Evening Echo
Curtain Call Nominated "Best Production 2000"

ISBN 1 902843 06 1
KS 2&3

Wacky Soap – The Music Score and Mini Musical
by Mark Wheeller and James Holmes

Mini-Musical Duration: 40 mins

A **Past-performance CD** gives you the opportunity to hear the songs of the play, while a fully orchestrated **Backing track CD** will be invaluable to those who want to produce the play but do not have music facilities.

"Wacky Soap' was an outstanding success!!!... We have had letters from people in the audience saying what a fab show it was and how impressed they were.

The most frequent comment was that it was a 'risk' to put it on as a school show (as opposed to doing 'Oliver' or 'Little Shop of Horrors') and one that thoroughly paid off!! 'The feel good factor was amazing' was another comment we had.

Many people said how impressed they were by the 'community' spirit of the production – everybody working together without the 'star' element creeping in!"

John Plant, Head of Drama, Southmoor School, Sunderland

The Story of Wacky Soap
by Mark & Rachel Wheeller
Illustrations by Geoffrey Greiggs

ISBN 1 902843 07 X

A beautifully illustrated book with the story of Wacky Soap in prose form.
It is often used as inspiration with props and costumes for when producing the play.

Other Plays by Mark Wheeller (not published by *dbda*)

Arson About
Script: Mark Wheeller (Ed. Andy Kempe)
Duration: 75 mins
Cast: 4 (2f & 2m with doubling)
Published by: Nelson Thornes Ltd. Tel: 01242 267100

Mollie and Ian are hot for each other. Stueey can be a real bright spark. Mr Butcher's comments have inflamed Shuttle. All in all it's combustible material but when you play with fire it can be more than your fingers that get burnt. Alrson About is a theatrical power keg which crackles with wit and moves along with a scorching pace. But in this play by Mark Wheeller the cost of 'arson about' becomes all too clear.

Chunnel of Love
Script: Graham Cole & Mark Wheeller
Duration: 100 mins
Cast: 25 (11f, 8m & 6m/f)
Published by: Zig Zag Education. Tel: 0117 950 3199

A bi-lingual play (80% English & 20% French) about teenage pregnancy. Lucy is fourteen - she hopes to become a vet and is working hard to gain good grades in her GCSE exams, when she discovers she is pregnant. She faces a series of major decisions, not least of which is what to tell the father... Ideal as a school production and Key Stage 4 Drama course book.

Sweet FA !
Script: Mark Wheeller
Duration: 45 mins plus interval
Cast: 3f / 2m (or more)
Published by: SchoolPlay Productions Ltd. Tel: 01206 540111

A Zigger Zagger for girls (and boys)! A new play (also available as a full length Musical) telling the true life story of Southampton girl footballer Sarah Stanbury (Sedge) whose ambition is to play Football (Soccer) for England. Her dad is delighted ... her mum disapproves strongly! An ideal GCSE production and Key Stage 4 Drama course book. Drama GCSE scheme of work also available.

Blackout – One Evacuee in Thousands   MUSICAL
Script: Mark Wheeller with the Stantonbury Youth Theatre   **Music:** Mark Wheeller
Duration: 90 mins plus interval   **Published by:** SchoolPlay Productions Ltd.

A Musical about the plight of Rachel Eagle, a fictional evacuee in World War II. Rachel's parents are determined that the war will not split the family up. After refusing to have her evacuated in 1939 they decide to do so midway though 1940. At first Rachel does not settle but, after the death of her mother, she becomes increasingly at home with her billets in Northamptonshire. When her father requests that she return she wants to stay where she feels at home. An ideal large scale school production with good parts for girls (and boys).

The Most Absurd Xmas (Promenade?) Musical in the World... Ever!
Script: Lyndsey Adams, Michael Johnston, Stuart White & Mark Wheeller   **Cast:** Big!
Music: James Holmes   **Duration:** 100 mins
Published by: SchoolPlay Productions Ltd. Tel: 01206 540111

Eat your heart out Ionesco! If you want a musical with a message ... don't consider this one! Santa fails to arrive one year in the Bower of Bliss. Why not? A shortage of carrots perhaps? Or is it because the central character is forbidden to use her musical gift, and whose parents disguise her as a cactus? It all ends reasonably happily and is a bundle of laughs. Originally conceived as a Promenade production. An ideal large scale school Christmas production or alternative an "absurd" summer production.

For more details and an up-to-date list of plays, please visit Mark's website:
www.amdram.co.uk/wheellerplays *(please note wheeller has two "l")*